MW00461296

LOVE

COLORING BOOK

Lindsey Boylan

DOVER PUBLICATIONS, INC.
MINEOLA, NEW YORK

Bibliographical Note

Love Coloring Book: Your Passport to Calm is a new work, first published by
Dover Publications, Inc., in 2016.

International Standard Book Number
ISBN-13: 978-0-486-81074-4
ISBN-10: 0-486-81074-7

Manufactured in the United States by RR Donnelley
81074701   2016
www.doverpublications.com

bliss

\\'blis\\

noun

1. supreme happiness; utter joy or contentment

2. heaven; paradise

3. your passport to calm

Take a romantic journey to a world of relaxation with *BLISS Love Coloring Book: Your Passport to Calm*. If you're a hopeless romantic, this treasury will keep your head in the clouds with its 46 ready-to-color designs of hearts, flowers, butterflies, and other images proving that love is in the air. Now you can travel to your newly found retreat of peace and serenity whenever you'd like with this petite-sized collection of sophisticated artwork.

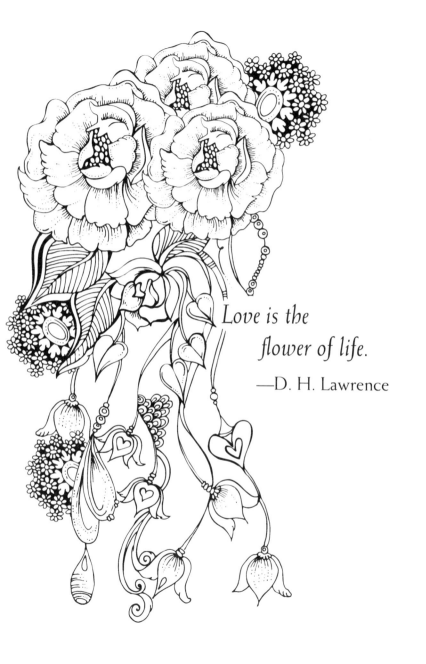

Love is the
flower of life.
—D. H. Lawrence

To love
beauty is
to see light.
—Victor Hugo

Love is wise;

Hatred is foolish.

—Bertrand Russell